Really Gross Science Experiments

HANDS-ON GROSSOLOGY

by
Sylvia Branzei
illustrated by
Jack Keely

PSS!
PRICE STERN SLOAN

This book is dedicated to Jess Brallier and to Chris Sykes for your numerous insights and your unending support.
–S.B. and J.K.

Trademark note: All terms mentioned in this book that are known to be registered trademarks, trademarks, or service marks of third parties have been appropriately capitalized when we are aware of them. Price Stern Sloan cannot attest to the accuracy of this information. The use of a term in this book should not be regarded as affecting the validity of any registered trademark, trademark, or service mark.

Library of Congress Cataloging-in-Publication Data

Branzei, Sylvia.
Hands-on grossology / by Sylvia Branzei ; illustrated by Jack Keely
p. cm. – (Grossology series)
Summary: Instructions for a variety of simple experiments that illustrate some of the more "disgusting" aspects of human physiology. Also includes related activities and experiments.
1. Human physiology—Experiments—Juvenile literature. 2. Biology—Experiments—Juvenile literature. 3. Body fluids—Experiments—Juvenile literature. [1. Human physiology—Experiments. 2. Biology—Experiments. 3. Body fluids—Experiments. 4. Experiments.] I. Keely, Jack, ill. II. Title. III. Series.

QP37.B8279 2003
612—dc21

2002193142

ISBN 0-8431-0305-1 A B C D E F G H I J

PSS!® and Grossology® are registered trademarks of Penguin Group (USA) Inc.

And Now a Message from Our Corporate Lawyer:

"Neither the Publisher nor the Authors shall be liable for any damage that may be caused or sustained as a result of conducting any of the activities in this book without specifically following instructions, conducting the activities without proper supervision, or ignoring the cautions contained in the book."

Table of Grosstents

Gross Experiments from All Around 52

Dear Reader...

"Grossology" is the science of really gross things. And "grossologists" are people who study really gross things. If you like gross stuff, you can become a grossologist. Stinky stuff, slimy stuff, smelly stuff, crusty stuff, rotten stuff and oozy stuff are all areas of study for a budding grossologist.

For a grossologist, finding out about gross stuff is very fulfilling, like: "A long time ago, people actually thought that the snot running from your nose during a cold was your brain leaking."

Finding out about gross stuff also involves using new words. To help you become a great grossologist, I might use words that confuse or stump you. Strange new words like "polymer" have been boldfaced and italicized; like this: ***polymer.***

To help you in your pursuit of the grossologist way, these words have been collected into a Gross Glossary on page 75.

Sharing gross information with others is also exciting. For example, "Hey Mom, did you know that you can actually buy jewelry made out of quail droppings? So I guess I know what I can give you for your birthday."

But what's most fun of all is getting your hands on gross stuff. I mean, really getting your hands on it! So what are you waiting for? Turn to page 8. Get gross!

Grossly yours,

Sylvia Branzei

The Peristalsis Pinch

If you lie on the ground, remove your ***small intestine***, and place it next to your body, it'll be four times longer than you!

Your small intestine collects nutrients from your food. Your ***large intestine*** sucks up water and creates little individual poops. ***Peristalsis***, which moves the stuff along, comes from the Greek words *peri* ("to wrap around") and *stal* ("to place"). The intestinal muscles wrap around, pinch, and release the poop, moving it along your gut tubes until the stuff's placed at the end. And you know where that is.

What you need:

hollow, flexible rubber tube *but not* a garden hose (a hollow plastic jump rope or a long balloon with both ends cut off also work)

funnel

tablespoon

cooking oil

marble

When you swallow, peristalsis is how food moves down your throat, or esophagus, to your stomach. So, peristalsis brings food into one end and takes it out the other end.

What you do:

- Make sure that the tube (imagine that this is your large intestine) is large enough for the marble to easily fit inside.
- Hold tube over a sink.
- Place funnel into one end of the tube. Pour 2 tablespoons of cooking oil (this is like the mucus that lines your large intestine) through the tube.
- Place tube in a horseshoe shape on a flat surface.
- Insert the marble (that's right, this is your poop) into one end of the tube. Pinch tube behind the marble. The marble moves forward.
- Continue. When marble reaches last bend of tube, it's time for a ***peristaltic rush***. Press tube behind the marble and just keep pushing until the marble ejects out the opening.

If your marble's stuck in the tube, try a smaller marble or a wider tube, or apply more oil to the tube's inside.

A doctor that specializes in problems of the ***rectum*** and ***anus*** is called a proctologist. *Proct* means "rectum" and *logos* means "study of."

Fake Blisters

Walk a mile in new shoes and you get a friction blister. Play in the sun at the beach and you get tiny burn blisters. Come down with chicken pox and you get tiny blisters (known as ***vesicles***). Touch poison oak and you get lots of blisters (Blister City!). Acquire a certain virus and you get a blister on your lip (known as a *cold sore*). Lots of stuff can cause your body to leak body fluid between two layers of your skin (in other words, a ***blister***).

And whatever you do, don't pop 'em (or you could end up with an oozing ***infection***).

What you need:

red food coloring

petroleum jelly

bowl

yellow food coloring

a white tissue

Blister beetles—which secrete a liquid that causes blisters—have been caught, ground up, and used medicinally to cause skin to blister.

What you do:

- Select a blister site (your hand, arm, or shin are good places).
- Place a drop of red food coloring on your finger and smear it onto the blister site in the shape and size of an "oval" quarter.
- Place a fingerful of the jelly into bowl; add small drop of yellow food coloring; mix until jelly is slightly yellow.
- Glob yellowish jelly mixture into center of red oval; mold jelly mixture into blister shape.
- Separate tissue into single layer.
- Tear tissue to the size of the red oval on your skin.
- Lay tissue over blister glob.
- *Gently* smear *clear* jelly over the tissue until it becomes invisible. *Carefully* tear away extra tissue.
- Clean off excess jelly on your skin.
- Be sure to show a parent the blister and painfully moan, "Look at this! See? I do need those really expensive sneakers."

What's Up

If your blister doesn't look real, try less yellow food coloring on your next blister, or try making a smaller blister—yours may be too big (a medium blister looks more realistic than a huge blister).

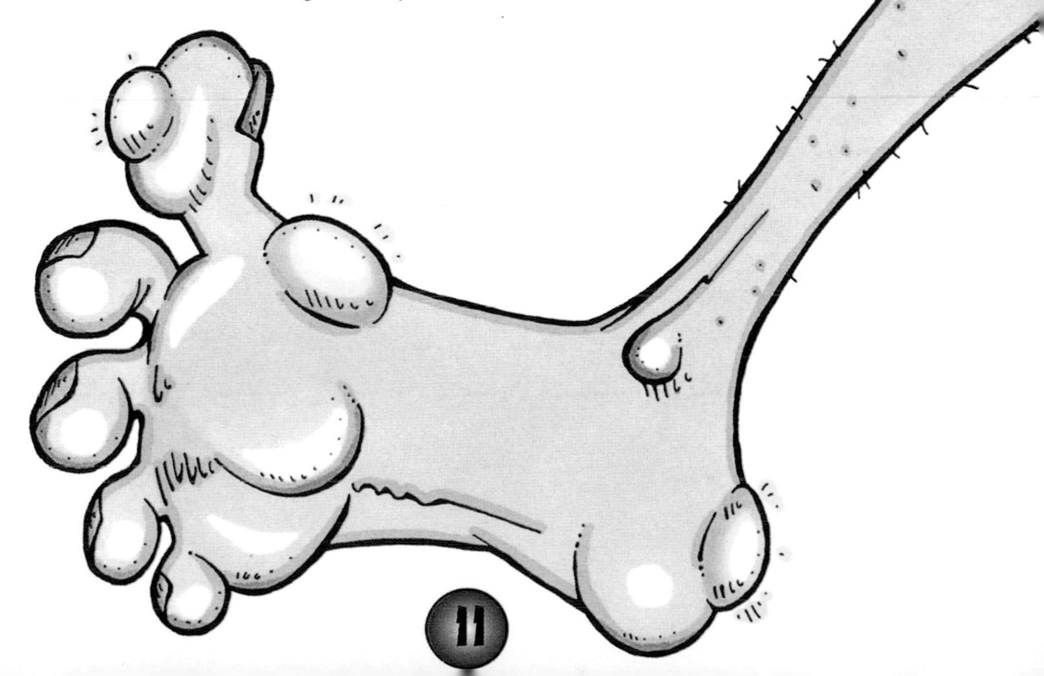

Fake Wounds

A wound can be a cut—*Ouch*, a scrape—*Arggh*, an abrasion—*Ack*, a laceration—*Eeeeow*, or a puncture—*Yikes*.

A wound must be cared for properly. Wash it with soap and water, flush with clean water, and swab around the wound with rubbing alcohol. If there's dirt in the wound, drip hydrogen peroxide into it. Cover it with a breathable bandage (air is good for wounds). And lastly, leave it alone.

Oh yeah, and make sure that you've had your ***tetanus*** shot. When you were a wee babe, you probably had three shots for tetanus. Tetanus ***vaccinations*** stop you from getting tetanus, also called ***lockjaw*** (a disease that's a lot less fun than a vaccination). You'll need to get a tetanus booster every few years.

Now here's the game plan for your next *owie*.

What you need:

petroleum jelly

bowl

red food coloring

powdered cocoa

a white tissue

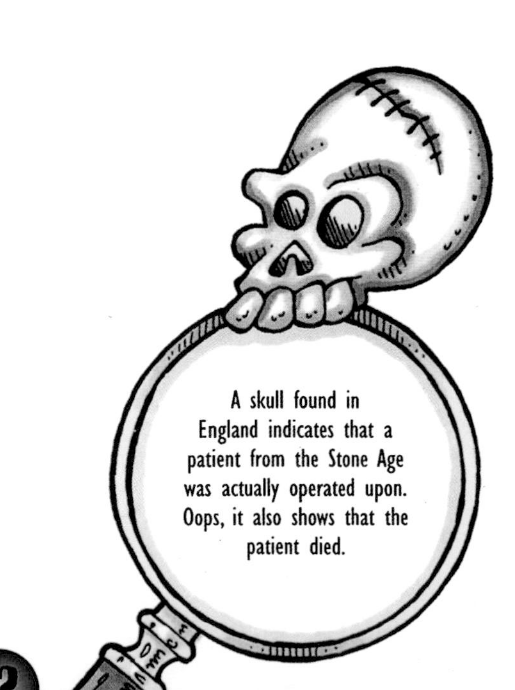

A skull found in England indicates that a patient from the Stone Age was actually operated upon. Oops, it also shows that the patient died.

What you do:

- Place fingerful of jelly into a bowl.
- Add 4 drops food coloring and pinch of cocoa. Mix well.
- Separate tissue into single layer.
- Rip out a 3-inch by 2-inch rectangle of tissue.
- Place tissue at wound site.
- Cover tissue with colored jelly.
- Mold tissue to form the wound's edges (sides of a wound are higher than its center).
- Rub sprinkled cocoa onto the wound's edges to make the edges dark, as though a scab is forming.
- Share your wound with someone easily grossed out.

What's Up

Making the perfect wound takes time and practice. However, the results can be so gruesome and Hollywood-like that it's worth the time. If your jelly looks like red gelatin, stir in a pinch more cocoa powder to make it opaque, like real blood. Think of a cut when shaping the tissue: the center is bloody mucky and the tissue ridges along the outside are your ripped skin.

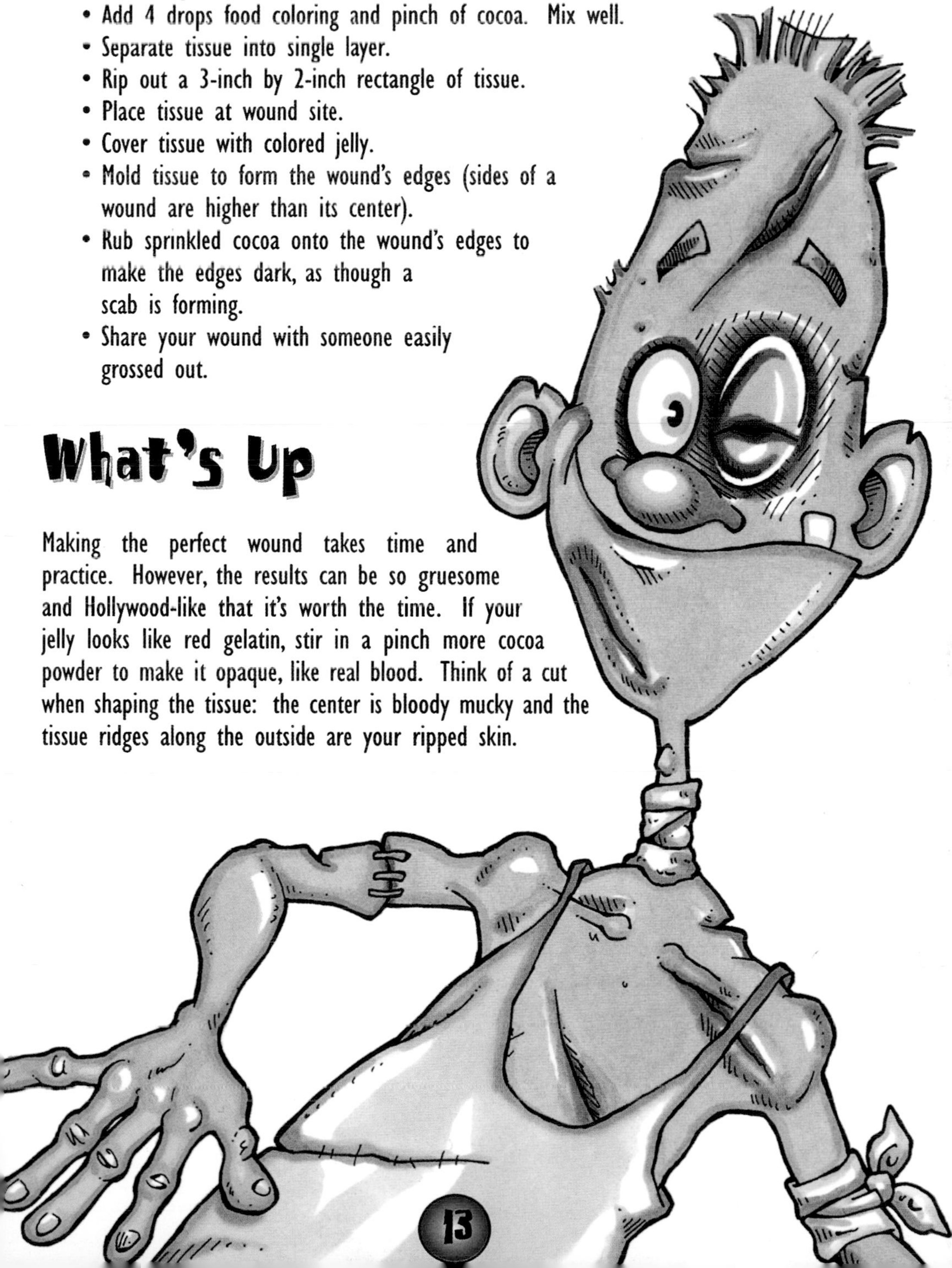

Phony Poo

How can you tell the difference between a pet dog's poop and a wild dog's turd? In a wild dog's poop, you'll notice little bones and fur; but because pet food doesn't include all this rough stuff, your dog's dookie is smoother. How about porcupine doo doo? Because porcupines chew on bark, their pellets look like dry clumps of sawdust.

By studying the "calling cards" left behind, you can tell which animals live in an area, changes in their diets, population density, and the location of their homes. Because ***scat*** (mammal dookie) can carry disease, **leave interactive poo-exploring to the poo experts!** That's right, there are people who are actually poo experts. Or, better yet, make your own "fake" poo.

What you need:

measuring cup

oatmeal (*not* instant)

cocoa powder

2 plates

teaspoon

fake sugar (like NutraSweet or Sweet'n Low; regular or powdered sugar will *not* work)

water

toilet paper

Every day 50 million dogs in the United States dump about 20 million pounds of poop. That's a whole lot of pooper scooping.

What you do:

- Place 1/2 cup oatmeal on plate; grind oatmeal with your fingers to make it less chunky.
- Add 2 teaspoons cocoa; mix with fingers.
- Add 2 teaspoons sugar; mix.
- Add water little by little until oatmeal mixture can be molded.
- Shape mixture into turd. Set masterpiece aside.
- On second plate, measure 3 teaspoons cocoa.
- Add 1 teaspoon sugar; mix.
- Roll fake turd in cocoa-sugar mixture.
- Place it on toilet paper and show it to your little brother. BUT!—DON'T FORGET TO LET HIM KNOW THAT IT IS NOT REAL!

What's Up

Real sugar melts in the water, making mixture too soft to mold. If you used *fake* sugar and still had problems, adjust the amount of water: too wet or too dry and it can't be molded. If it still doesn't form, be sure you're not using *instant* oatmeal.

Belch Model

What's the difference between a burp and a belch? To some people, they're the same thing; to others a belch is a series of burps. So, it's burp and BELLLLLCH. Either way, burps and belches are air escaping from the stomach through the throat.

Inside your stomach is a little pocket of air. When this air becomes squeezed, or when you add extra gas from drinking carbonated drinks or talking fast, you belch. In both of these cases, your stomach does nothing to create new gas.

If you take an ***antacid*** or sodium bicarbonate for an upset stomach, you may belch like crazy. Now you've actually *produced* gas in your stomach. Your stomach excretes lots of ***acid*** to break down food. When you're uncomfortable with too much of that acid, you might take an antacid. When the chemicals in the antacid react with the acids in your stomach, gas is created. The gas builds up and up until you just can't hold it anymore. BEELLLLLLLLCH.

What you need:

vinegar

medium or larger balloon

funnel

baking soda

teaspoon

Heartburn is when stomach acids go up your throat and into your mouth (yuck!). *Anti* means "against"; so *antacid* means "against the acid."

What you do:

The first thing is DO THIS *MESSY* EXPERIMENT OVER A SINK!

- Pour 2 teaspoons of vinegar into the bottom of balloon (your stomach).
- Place funnel into neck of balloon; add 1 heaping teaspoon of baking soda to the balloon stomach.
- Very quickly close the balloon by pinching its neck (your esophagus).
- Watch your balloon stomach expand with gas.
- Stretch and slightly unpinch the esophagus to release gas (belch!).
- Keep practicing the pinch release until you can make the belch model sound like a real burp.

What's Up

If you don't pinch the balloon quickly enough, bubbling liquid may rush up from the throat of your balloon and out the mouth. Whoa! To slow down the bubbling, add less vinegar and baking soda.

URP!

Bogus Blood

Some people actually faint at the sight of blood. Which is sort of odd because everybody, including fainters, has about five quarts of blood rushing through their bodies. If it weren't for this wonderful stuff, oxygen would not get to all the parts of your body and you would die. Yep, blood is life.

You think of blood as being red. Yet actually less than half of your blood is made of red blood cells (called ***erythrocytes***). The "red" in red blood cells comes from a pigment called hemoglobin. ***Hemoglobin*** has iron molecules, which cruise around your body exchanging much-needed oxygen for useless carbon dioxide.

What you need:

clear corn syrup (the kind used for cooking, not for pancakes)

measuring cup

bowl

water

tablespoon

red food coloring

cornstarch

powdered cocoa

Quick!—
Name the strongest muscle in your body. Nope, not your biceps. It's your heart.

• • •

Maybe you've heard the saying, "Blood is thicker than water." It's true! Blood is almost five times thicker than water.

What you do:

- In a bowl, mix 1/4 cup syrup and 2 tablespoons water. Stir well.
- Add 4 drops red food coloring. Stir.
- Add 2 tablespoons cornstarch and 1/2 tablespoon powdered cocoa. Stir very, very, very well.
- NOW PUT ON SOME REALLY WORTHLESS CLOTHING! THIS STUFF WILL *STAIN* YOUR CLOTHES. MAKE SURE THAT AN ADULT AGREES THAT THE CLOTHES ARE "WORTHLESS."
- Drip the blood from the side of your mouth. Or, better yet, put some in your mouth (it's not harmful, but tastes pretty lousy).
- Sneak up on an unsuspecting person and whisper, "I vant to suck your blood."

What's Up

If your blood's lumpy, further mix the cornstarch and cocoa. More cornstarch makes it thicker; more water makes it runnier. You can safely store your blood in a resealable bag.

WARNING!

REMEMBER: DON'T DRIP THE BLOOD ON ANYTHING—FURNITURE, CARPETING, STUFF LIKE THAT—THAT COULD GET YOU INTO BIG TROUBLE!

Every day more than 1,000 gallons of blood are pumped through your body. Imagine that the next time you see gallons of milk lined up at the grocery store.

The snot (or mucus) that constantly coats your throat and sometimes leaks from your nose is made of ***polymer*** molecules that are long and stretchy (which is why snot is such great stuff). Because glue is also made of polymers, it's the perfect ingredient for fake snot.

Your own snot is actually clear, until you get a cold—then your nose mucus becomes a *lovely* green color. The green comes from dead ***bacteria*** and bacterial waste. Have a snotty time.

What you need:

Borax laundry booster
(No other detergent will do!)

measuring cup

tap water

clean, empty 1 liter/quart soda bottle

Elmer's glue
(No other kind will do!)

tablespoon

green food coloring

What you do:

- Mix 1/8 cup Borax laundry booster and 1/2 liter *warm* water in soda bottle. Shake until most of the borax dissolves (all of it won't dissolve, and that's OK). Let this solution cool to *room temperature*.
- Place 4 tablespoons of glue into a cup.
- Add 4 tablespoons of water. Stir.
- Add 2 drops of green food coloring. Stir well.
- Measure 3 tablespoons of borax solution from the soda bottle and add to glue mixture in cup; stir until the mixture looks like a clump of snot in a pool of water.
- Reach into the cup, remove your snot, fake a sneeze—AAACHOOOO!—and show your friends how much snot came out of your nose. WARNING: DO NOT PUT THE FAKE SNOT *IN* YOUR NOSE!

What's Up

The glue is a long and stretchy polymer molecule. The Borax is also a special type of molecule called a ***cross linker.*** If you think of the glue as being like the sides of a ladder, then the borax is like the rungs of the ladder. So the Borax pulls the glue together to make it lumpy. If your fake snot was too runny, then you didn't add enough of the cross linker (Borax).

If it was too lumpy, you added too much Borax.

Fake Edible Barf

People were recently asked, "What's the most disgusting thing your body does?" The number one answer was, *ta dah*, VOMIT! Yep, good old barf is really repulsive. However, if it weren't for upchucking, you might not be here reading about it. Vomiting is very important because it gets rid of germs and other contaminants that your body can't handle. So the next time you upchuck, don't forget to thank yourself.

Now imagine barf that is not only fake but edible . . .

What you need:

- **oatmeal**
- **tablespoon**
- **applesauce**
- **frying pan**
- **powdered cocoa**
- **spatula**
- **plastic or glass plate**
- **mixing bowl**
- **raisin bran cereal**
- **measuring cup**
- **1 packet unflavored gelatin**
- **yellow food coloring**

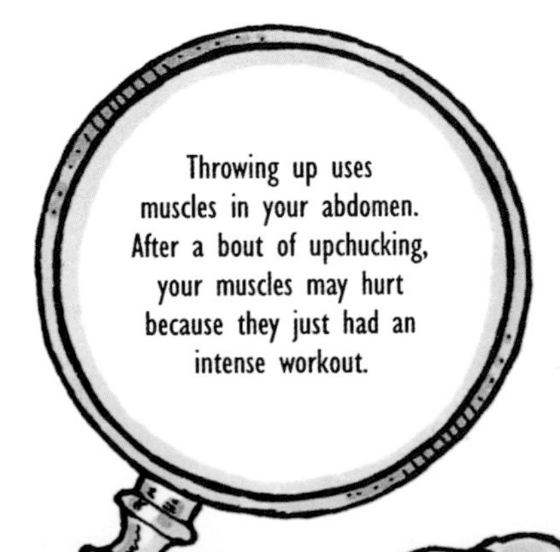

What you do:

- Put a fistful of oatmeal into bowl. With the spoon, crunch the oatmeal.
- Add a fistful of raisin bran cereal and crunch with the spoon.
- WARNING! GET AN ADULT!
- Got an adult? Great! Place 1/4 cup applesauce into the frying pan on medium heat.
- When the applesauce begins to bubble, add 1 packet gelatin and stir well.
- Add 1 to 2 pinches powdered cocoa and stir thoroughly.
- Turn off heat.
- Sprinkle a small amount of the oatmeal-and-cereal mixture into the pan.
- Add 2 drops of yellow food coloring.
- Stir the mixture a bit (stir too much and all the really gross chunky bits will disappear).
- With the spatula, scrape the barf onto a plate.
- Spread and shape it until the barf looks real.
- Cool for several hours.
- Use spatula to remove barf from plate.
- Gross out your auntie by eating to your stomach's delight!

What's Up

The gelatin joined the applesauce and cereal bits into one mass. The cocoa powder does not add taste but changes the color of the applesauce to a lovely brown.

Fake Dookie Cookies

There's an old saying that goes, "Waste not, want not." But if you didn't make waste—*your* solid waste (known as "poop")—you'd be wishing that you did.

An animal that can't poop is said to be constipated. ***Constipation*** is not a good thing. Pooping is a good thing. For example, because the little mites that live in your eyelash roots can't poop, they live a very short life. Pooping is important because it gets rid of stuff that your body doesn't need.

What you need:

measuring cups
bowl
saucepan
mixing spoon
powdered cocoa
white sugar
flour
rolled oats
shredded wheat or wheat flake cereal
green food coloring
measuring spoons
baking tray
oven
margarine
brown sugar
vanilla

During colonial times, a person had to walk down the street very carefully. Since there were no indoor toilets, chamber pots filled with pee and poo were just dumped from the window and onto the street: "Look out below!"

What you do:

WARNING! GET AN ADULT!

- In saucepan, melt a mixture of 1/2 cup margarine, 1/2 cup white sugar, and 4 teaspoons cocoa. Set aside.
- In mixing bowl, add 1/2 cup brown sugar (packed), 1 egg, 1/2 teaspoon vanilla, 1 cup flour, 3/4 cup rolled oats. Stir well.
- Add melted cocoa mixture. Stir well.
- Add a little squirt of green food coloring and mix.
- Add 1/2 cup of cereal and mix. (If using shredded wheat, crumble it first.)
- Shape the dough into turds. You can make flattened cow pies or little kitty turds. Remember that cookie dough will flatten a bit during baking.
- Warm oven to 375°. Place cookies on baking tray and put into oven. Bake 9 to 11 minutes. Remove, USING POTHOLDERS. PLACE ON A SAFE SURFACE TO COOL.
- To serve, it looks best (grossest!) to place a single cookie on a plate or napkin.
- Find someone who didn't smell cookies baking and say, "Hey, want a yummy treat?"

What's Up

Make all of the cookies on each pan the same size. If you place giant cow pies and little kitty turds on the same pan, the kitty poop cookies will burn before the cow pie cookies are done. Cookie dough that's too crumbly means there wasn't enough moisture. Add a little bit of milk or a couple tablespoons of melted butter until the dough will form into little turds or cow pies. If your dough was too runny, add more flour, bit by bit, until the dough can be shaped.

Pee Pee Capacity

To pee or not to pee? Don't waste your time asking—you *have* to pee.

Urine is one way that your body gets rid of waste. Your ***kidneys*** decide what stuff in your blood to keep and what to ditch: "Too much water; out goes the water! Need that sugar; sugar stays here!" (This blood filtering process occurs every 30 minutes throughout your entire life.)

What your body doesn't want goes into your bladder, the storage unit for your urine. When your ***bladder*** is full you say, "Wow, I gotta take a leak."

What you need:

1/2-cup measuring cup

empty plastic container (a peanut butter jar or large yogurt container works well)

a permanent marker

pencil

paper

soap

privacy

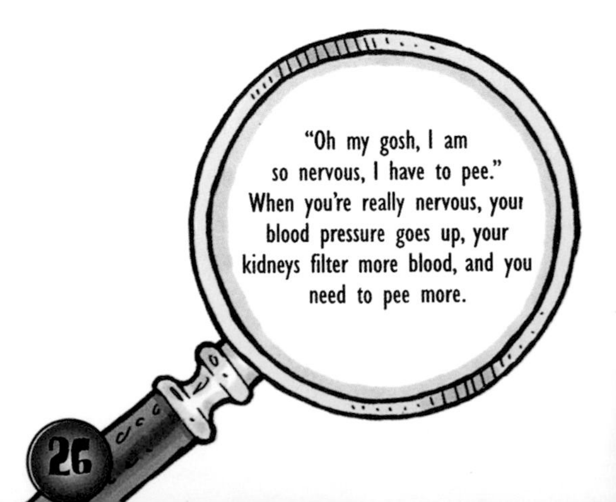

What you do:

FIRST THING, TALK TO A PARENT! YOU'RE GOING TO EXPERIMENT WITH PEE. PARENTS MUST KNOW ABOUT AND AGREE TO THINGS LIKE THIS.

- Pour 1/2 cup of water into the plastic container. With the marker, make a line on the container at the 1/2-cup level. Continue to pour and mark half-cup amounts on the container until you reach its top.
- Start your experiment first thing the next morning: pee into the container. Using the paper and pencil, record the amount you peed and the date and time of the pee.
- CAREFULLY pour the urine into the toilet, then wash out the container VERY WELL.
- Pee pee is kind of like milk. New pee is very clean. However, after it sits around for a bit, bacteria will collect and make it go bad.
- Wash your hands with soap (CAREFULLY!).
- Continue to record your pee amounts for the whole day.
- Total the day's pee output.
- The next day drink lots and lots and lots of water. Again, keep track of your pee output.

What's Up

The day you drank lots of water, you probably made more pee. However, if it was a really hot day, your body may have gotten rid of some water through sweating. Your pee output depends on how much you drink, the weather, and your activities.

When you have a stuffed-up nose, food just doesn't taste so great. In fact, it doesn't taste at all.

This is because your nose and your mouth work together to help you taste. The inside of your nose, mouth, throat, and ears are interconnected.

For example, the tiny molecules from a baking birthday cake float through the air. You breathe them in. The cake molecules enter in through your nose and pass over the back of your tongue. They dissolve in your ***saliva*** and—yummy!—you actually taste the cake without putting it in your mouth.

Or have you ever eaten something nasty and exclaimed, "This tastes poopy!" Then your bratty cousin responds, "How do you know? Have you eaten poop?!" Now, as a grossologist, you can explain to your bratty cousin how taste and smell are connected. So there!

Your mouth prepares for eating by making a whole bunch of saliva. Even before you swallow, your ***salivary glands*** dump saliva into your mouth. Your wonderful saliva helps to break down food into mush that you can swallow more easily.

Saliva mania is not limited to yummy smells. Your friendly saliva also gushes at bitter or sour smells to lessen the shock of the yuck that you're about to get stuck with. Thank you, spit!

a container of lemon juice or vinegar

What you do:

- Open the container of lemon juice or vinegar.
- Stick your nose close to the spout and inhale deeply. Don't suck up the liquid—just smell!
- Notice what happens inside your mouth.

What's Up

If your mouth didn't water like crazy, you probably have a stuffed-up nose.

Try the experiment on several volunteers. For this experiment, first blindfold each person. Then try several different liquids, such as water, soda, milk, or iced tea. Then try the lemon or vinegar juice. Ask the volunteer which liquid produced the most spit.

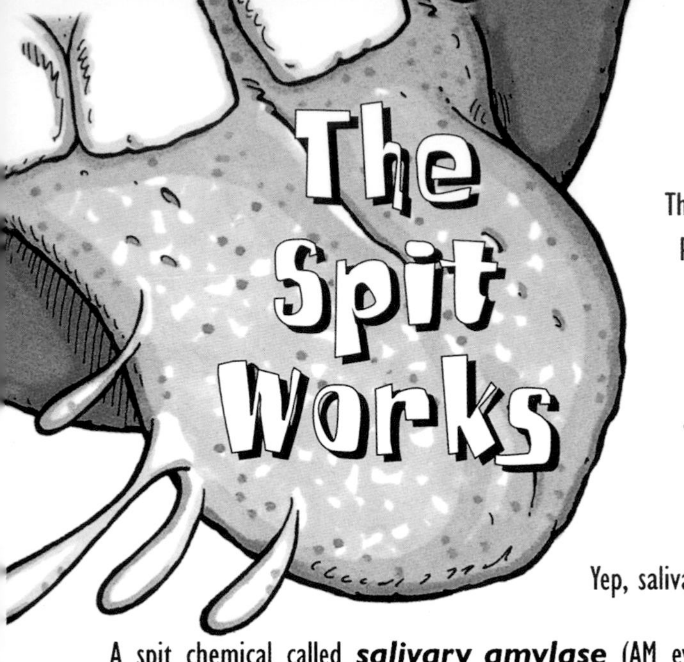

The Spit Works

The saliva that you produce (two pounds of it every day!) —

- makes food slippery for swallowing,
- dissolves food so that you can taste and enjoy it,
- kills bacteria, and
- begins preparing food for digestion by breaking down its chemical structure.

Yep, saliva is special.

A spit chemical called ***salivary amylase*** (AM eye lace) breaks down long ***starch*** molecules. Amylase goes to work on starchy food like cereals, rice, corn, or potatoes as soon as they enter your mouth. Starch molecules are really, really long and your body can't use them unless they are sliced into shorter pieces. Your spit changes the starch molecules into sweet sugar molecules. This way a plain hunk of bread is transformed into sugar. How sweet it is!

What you need:

2 crackers (unsalted is best)

2 glass bowls or small cups

liquid iodine (drugstores sell this in their first aid section.)

What you do:

- Crunch up one cracker into one of the glass containers.
- Add several drops of iodine. If the iodine turns black or dark blue, starch is present.
- Place the other cracker in your mouth. DO NOT EAT THE CRACKER WITH THE IODINE ON IT! IODINE CAN MAKE YOU SICK IF EATEN!
- Keep chewing until the cracker is all mushy. DON'T SWALLOW IT!
- Spit out the chewed cracker into the clean glass container.
- Add several drops of iodine. What color is the iodine?

What's Up

The iodine on the plain cracker probably turned very dark blue or black. Starch in the cracker caused the color change. However, iodine on the chewed cracker probably stayed brown or turned a dark purple. With the chewed cracker, there was much less starch to react with the iodine because your saliva had changed much of the starch into sugar.

If this didn't work, repeat the experiment but this time chew the cracker longer before adding the iodine. If this still doesn't work, repeat the experiment again. But this time, before adding iodine to the cracker, first add water to the iodine until it is a light brown or tan color.

The Great Wax Detector

Search someone's ear for wax. Everyone has at least a little bit of wax.

The outer ear canal—just inside the ear's opening to the outside world—has wax-making glands. The great thing about ear wax is that it traps unwanted gunk from the outside world.

Wax usually balls up, rolls to the ear's outer edge, then falls out. However, in some people, a batch of wax may harden in the ears. This wax must be removed by a doctor or with special ear wax medicine.

Let's check out this wax stuff.

What you need:

a half-liter plastic soda bottle (WARNING: DO NOT USE A SMALLER BOTTLE)

scissors

small flashlight

permanent marker

clear adhesive tape

a willing volunteer

What you do:

- Remove the cap of the plastic soda bottle.
- WARNING: YOU MUST HAVE AN ADULT HELP WITH THE SCISSORS AND CUTTING. Use the scissors to cut off the top part of the bottle. Get rid of the bottle's bottom. You won't need it.
- Trim the top of the bottle until it fits snugly onto the end of the flashlight.
- Coat the inside of the bottle top with permanent marker.
- Allow the marker to dry.
- Tape the bottle top to the end of the flashlight.
- Find a willing volunteer. You may need to promise to do something nice for your volunteer.
- To look into the ear, have your volunteer straighten his ear canal by pinching the back of his ear, then pulling it upward and toward the back of the head.
- Place your ear wax detector close to (NOT IN!) the opening of the ear canal. WARNING: NEVER PUT ANYTHING INTO AN EAR.
- Turn on the flashlight.
- Look for ear wax. The wax will either be sticky and honey-colored or gray and brittle.
- Say stuff like, "This is really disgusting!"

What's Up

No wax sighting? Maybe your volunteer has an undetectable amount of ear wax. Find another volunteer. Or maybe you need a new battery in the flashlight.

Oily Skin Test

Some people get zits and some people don't. That's just the way it is. Zits have nothing to do with wearing bangs or eating greasy food. Zits have a lot to do with how oily your skin is, which is determined by genetics. Basically, if your mom or dad had pimples, you will too. But don't go blaming your folks either, they got it from their parents, who got it from their parents, who got it from . . . . You get it!

Zits pop up on oily areas of skin. Oil is produced in little glands under the skin called ***sebaceous glands***. If the sebaceous glands squirt very little oil, you have dry skin. If the glands ooze a lot of oil, you have oily skin. To find out your oiliness factor (or your zit potential), try this:

What you need:

clean wash cloth

soap

water

rubbing alcohol

cotton swab

clock

small square of tissue paper

What you do:

- Use the wash cloth and soap to scrub your forehead.
- Use the cotton swab to clean the area with rubbing alcohol. (WATCH OUT! DO NOT DO THIS NEAR YOUR EYES!)
- Wait 4 hours. Do not touch your forehead during this time.
- After 4 hours, firmly smear the tissue across your forehead. If more than half of the paper has an oil mark, your skin is oily. If a light oil smudge is on the paper, your skin is normal. If there is no oil smudge, your skin is dry.

What's Up

This activity is fairly accurate in determining the oiliness of your skin. However, you may get false results if you perform it on a very hot day or if you exercise heavily during your 4-hour waiting period. On these occasions, your forehead may be covered in sweat, which would also wipe off on the tissue.

Even if you discover that your skin is dry, this does not mean that you won't ever get pimples. Almost 80 percent of all people get pimples at some time in their lives, especially during puberty. So, don't give up washing your face! Clean skin will help to control break-outs.

"Pardon me."

Belching is a natural and uncontrollable event. Although you can *eruct* (another word for "belch") quietly, the built-up gas in your stomach air pocket still escapes. For polite, silent burps most of the air is released from your nose. However, some people are belch champions. They really know how to let them fly. These people help to force the air out by using their stomach and throat muscles. BELCH! How lovely.

Burps occur spontaneously from the gas that enters your stomach while eating, drinking, and talking. However, you can actually cultivate a burp. Check this out to find out how.

What you need:

air

What you do:

- Pretend you are eating air soup and swallow a huge spoonful of air. You may want to do this several times.
- Now relax. Wait a minute or so and b-u-r-r-r-r-p.
- If it doesn't come out, relax even more by making the muscles in your shoulders and stomach go limp.
- Once you've mastered the Burp-o-Matic, you can learn to say entire burp sentences. Maybe even sing belch songs. Wow!—will your mom ever be glad that you learned this.

What's Up

OK, you swallowed a bunch of air, waited, and nothing came out. Try plugging your nose when you gulp air to be sure that it is going into your stomach and not out your nose. Still no good? Are you lying on your back? You can't burp when you are lying down. Or, after you swallow air, wait 30 seconds, then tighten your stomach muscles to help force the air out. As a last resort, try keeping your mouth closed. Suck in air through your nose. Swallow it down into your throat. Then force it back up your throat and out through your mouth. Yes!

Stench Quenchers

(a.k.a. "Deodorants")

"You have body odor." ACK!

In many modern cultures (yours included, probably) body odor is a no-no. People just don't want to be around people who stink. However, body odor (B.O.) is a human condition; we just can't help it. So humans use ***deodorants*** and ***antiperspirants*** to battle stench. Deodorant kills the bacteria that munch on sweat to make you stinky (that's right, B.O. is the smell of bacterial poop!). Antiperspirants, on the other hand, swell the muscles and blood vessels around sweat pores, causing the pores to fill up with sweat rather than send it out. Most people buy their B.O. battlers at the store. However, you can make your own stench quenchers at home.

What you need:

4 resealable bags (plastic baggies)

baking soda

tablespoon

cornstarch

talcum powder

A person with B.O.*

*Humans don't get body odor until they are around the age of 12 or 13, so you may have to get your teenage sister to help you out here.

When it comes to humans, "perspire" and "sweat" are both words for the exact same thing. Such as, "I'm perspiring like crazy" or "I'm sweating like crazy." But what's weird is that when it comes to nonliving objects, only "sweat" is used. Like, "It was so humid, the walls were sweating," not "It was so humid, the walls were perspiring."

What you do:

- Into one baggie, measure 2 tablespoons of baking soda. Label the bag "baking soda" (for labeling, you may want to use masking tape and a pen).
- Into another baggie, measure 2 tablespoons of cornstarch. Label the bag "cornstarch."
- Into the third bag, measure 2 tablespoons of talcum powder. Label the bag "talcum powder."
- Into the last bag, measure 1 tablespoon each of baking soda, cornstarch, and talcum powder. Label the bag "combination."
- In the morning, wash your armpits. Then rub some baking soda under each pit.
- Go about your day. At the close of the day, sniff your pits.
- Using a scale of 1 through 5, with 1 as "very excellent" and 5 as "it just doesn't work," record your rating on the baking soda bag.
- Repeat the daily procedure for the remaining homemade deodorants.
- Which deodorant worked best for you?

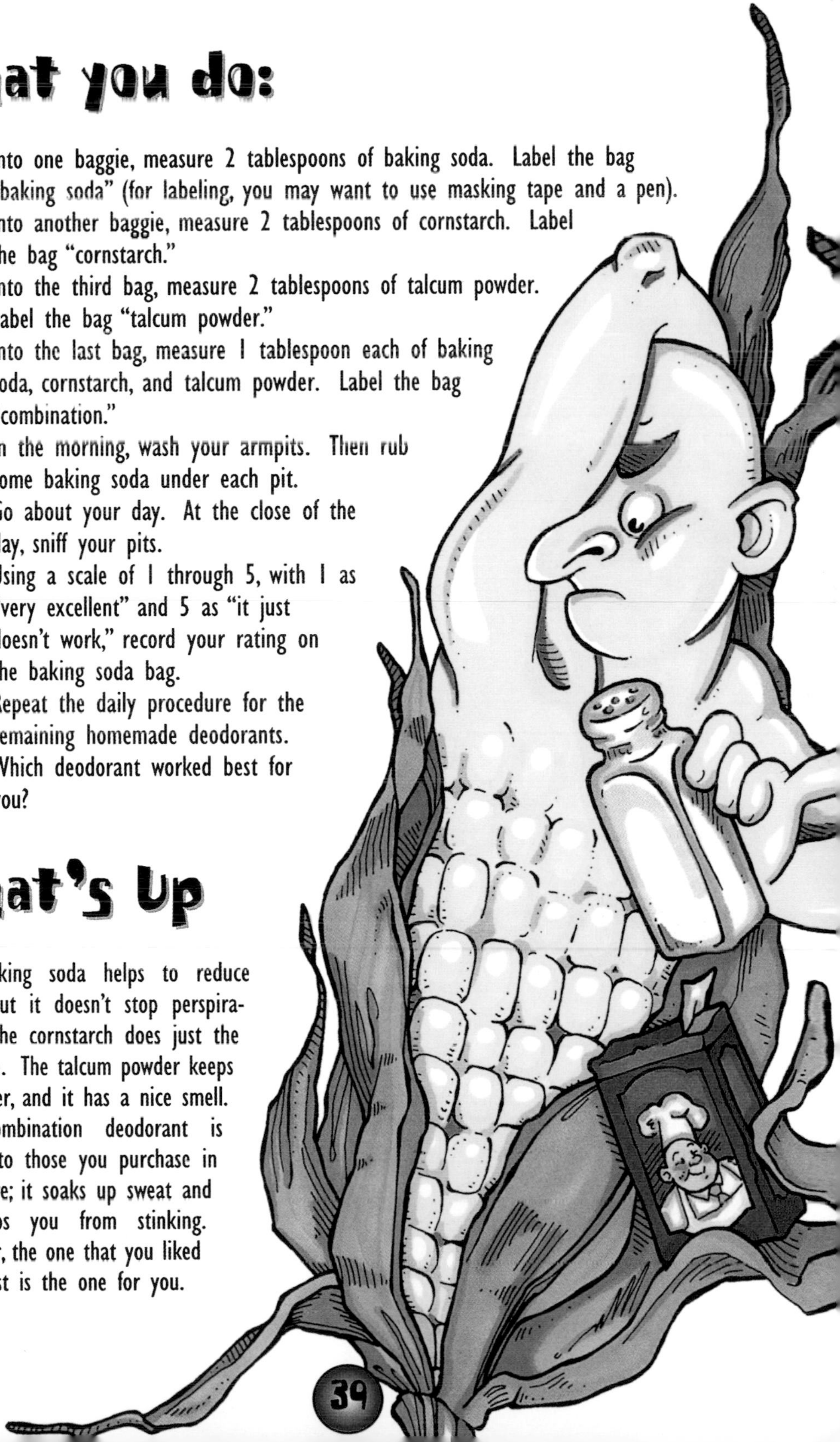

What's Up

The baking soda helps to reduce smell, but it doesn't stop perspiration. The cornstarch does just the opposite. The talcum powder keeps you drier, and it has a nice smell. The combination deodorant is closest to those you purchase in the store; it soaks up sweat and it keeps you from stinking. However, the one that you liked the most is the one for you.

Perfumed And Colorful Pee

Right now your body is making pee. Yep, even as you read these words. Every day, your kidneys filter about 180 quarts of blood. What your kidneys consider waste—the useless stuff—drips into your bladder. This pee is stored in the bladder until you pass it into the toilet. On an average day, you get rid of four to eight cups of pee (see experiment on page 26).

What's really neat is that sometimes the useless stuff adds color and smell to your urine. Go ahead, see if you can spruce up your pee.

What you need:

cooked asparagus

cooked beets

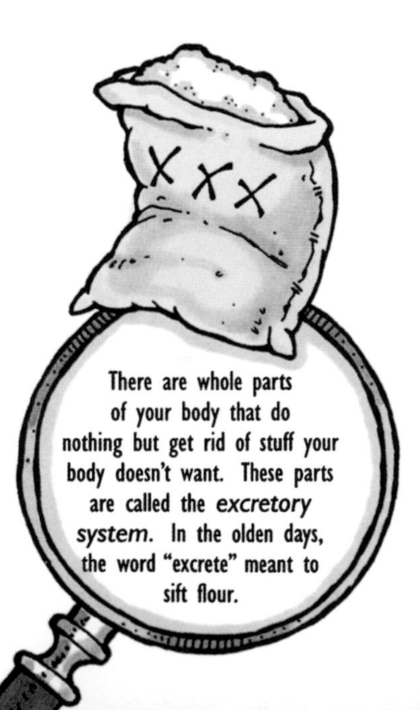
There are whole parts of your body that do nothing but get rid of stuff your body doesn't want. These parts are called the *excretory system*. In the olden days, the word "excrete" meant to sift flour.

What you do:

- Have an adult cook up a bunch of asparagus for you. Eat the stuff. (Your grandmother will be proud of you.)
- Go about your day.
- At pee time, pay attention to the odor of your urine. It may take several hours for the asparagus to do its work, so be patient.
- Have an adult cook up a bunch of beets for you. Eat the stuff. (Your grandmother will be shocked!)
- Go about your day.
- At pee time, check out the color of your urine. Once checked, don't forget to flush! It may take several hours for the beets to do their work, so be patient.
- If you're aiming to have both perfumed and colorful pee, try eating *both* beets and asparagus during a single meal.

What's Up

Don't despair if your asparagus pee had no odor. Not every person creates musky pee from eating asparagus. Maybe you are one of the lucky ones. (Or is it unlucky?) No pinkish or reddish urine from the beets? Oh well, maybe your pee-pee-making system isn't the kind that produces colorful pee. Or maybe you just didn't eat enough beets! If you want to experience a bright yellow pee, try taking some vitamin B. Maybe you'll find shocking yellow pee just as appealing.

Scabs are nature's bandage.

When you get a wound, your body looks after you by quickly stopping the bleeding and then forming a nice little dried-blood cover over the cut. How sweet! Remember, most minor wounds heal rather quickly—if you keep them clean and do **not** pick 'em!

To find out the rate of your healing process, try this experiment the next time you get an owie.

What you need:

yourself (when you get a little cut or scrape)

a watch

soap and water

bandage

calendar

pencil

WARNING!

This experiment is for minor cuts and scrapes only. In the case of a deep cut, go directly to an adult for help.

What you do:

- The next time you scrape or cut yourself, pull out your watch. (OK, OK, you can first say "Ouch!" and then turn to your watch!)
- Notice the time.
- Clean the wound with soap and water.
- Observe your wound.
- Time how long it takes for your wound to stop bleeding.
- Cover wound with a bandage.
- Mark date of your owie on calendar.
- Each day, observe your wound (remove bandage and replace with a clean one if necessary).
- On the calendar record when
  1) the scab first begins to form,
  2) the scab's edges begin to curl up, and
  3) the scab actually falls off. (No!—you can't help by picking at it.)
- How long did it take for your wound to heal?

What's Up

After six minutes, your minor wound will stop bleeding. The scab will probably form within two days. After several days to a week, the edges of the scab should begin to separate from your skin. And one or two days later, your scab will fall off. The entire experiment—from ACK! to "all better"—will last ten to fourteen days. Isn't it amazing how quickly our body makes us as good as new?

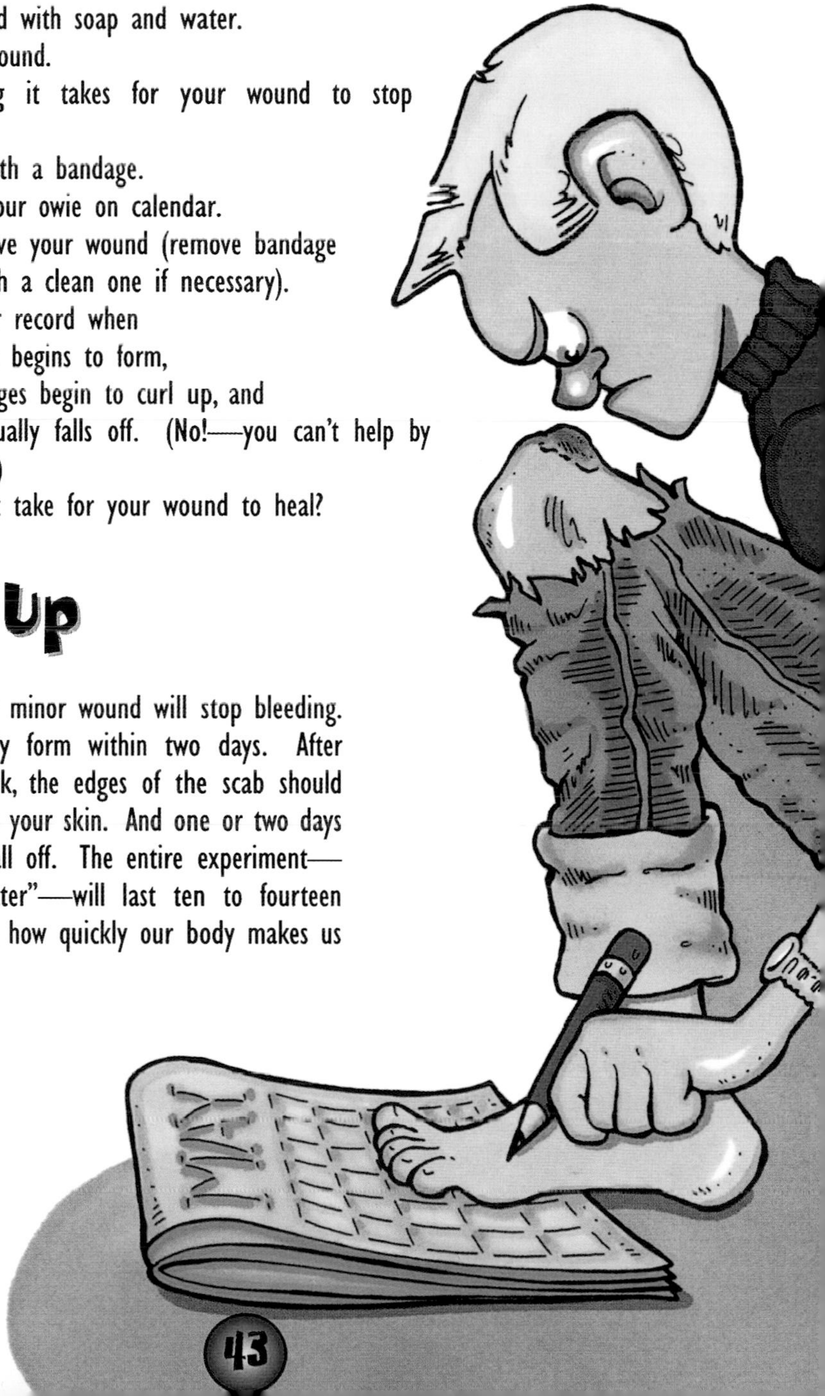

Plaque Check

Nope, the plaque in this experiment is not the award that hangs on your wall.

This ***plaque*** is the sticky film coating your teeth. Go ahead, run your tongue over your teeth. What you felt was a layer of bacteria that lives in your mouth. These bacteria especially enjoy hanging out at the base of your teeth, where they munch on leftover food bits. If left on their own, the bacteria cause cavities, decay, and gum disease.

When you brush your teeth, the bacteria are washed away—at least temporarily. Some hide in the micro-crevices of your teeth, only to reappear after the toothbrush attack. That is why you can't get away with brushing just for special occasions. Flossing is also important, because it gets those ugly bacteria that hunker down at the base of the teeth.

However, a swipe of the brush and a tug on the flossing string may not be good enough. Let's check out how successful a bacteria fighter you really are.

toothbrush

toothpaste

disclosing tablets (available from your dentist or at most drugstores)

water

Instead of brushing his teeth, Chairman Mao, the former dictator of China, rinsed his mouth with tea. Over the years, a lovely green film coated his teeth. What a smile!

What you do:

- Brush your teeth *normally* (not that fantastic brush job that you do just before going to the dentist).
- Chew a disclosing tablet.
- Use water to swish the tablet juices around in your mouth.
- Look in the mirror and smile. Argh!!!—*what's wrong with my mouth?*
- The disclosing tablets stick to the plaque where you didn't brush.
- I hope you like having a colorful smile for awhile. (Just kidding!) To remove the tablet stain—and the plaque you missed the first time around—brush your teeth again.

What's Up

Make sure you swish the dissolved disclosing tablet around your mouth. Otherwise, you will have coloring only in the area where you chewed. Also, after the experiment, carefully rinse your toothbrush bristles to remove all of the stain.

Heat Off!

When it's hot outside, you sweat. When you exercise, you sweat. And when you have a fever due to illness, you sweat.

Instead of saying "sweat," some people say "***perspiration***," because they think it sounds nicer. "Sweating" or "perspiring," it's the exact same thing: the oozing from little openings on your skin of water, salts, and a body waste called ***urea*** that is also found in urine.

Sweating is so important that your body has more than 2 million little holes (sweat glands) that together can ooze up to a quart of liquid per day. The number of sweat glands that you develop actually depends upon where you were raised as a baby. Infants raised in hot, tropical climates develop more sweat glands than infants from colder climates.

Think of sweating as your body's air conditioning system. Without the liquid squirting out to coat your skin, you would overheat, and that can *really* mess up your body. Let's find out how sweating helps to keep you cool.

What you need:

cotton ball

rubbing alcohol

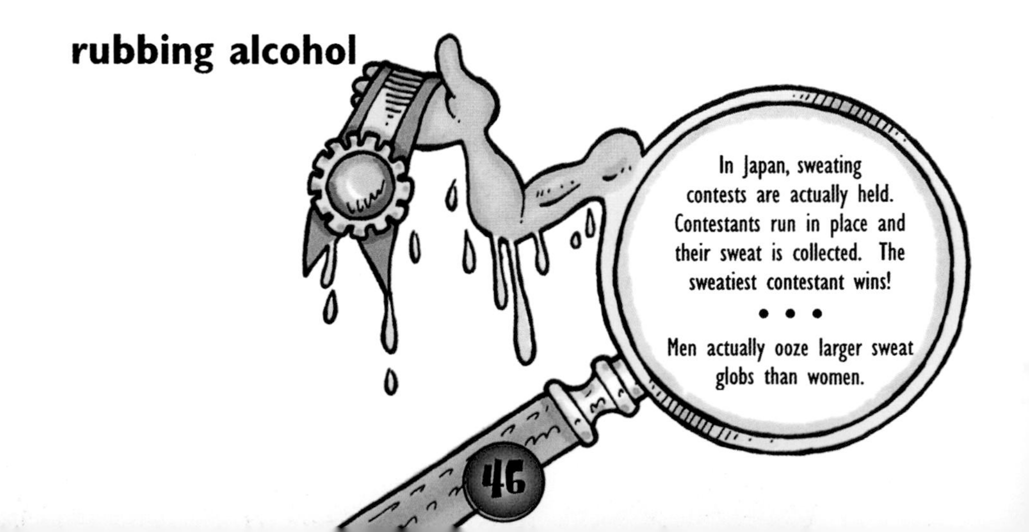

What you do:

- Wet cotton ball with rubbing alcohol.
- Wipe a forearm with the ball.
- Blow on the moist part of this forearm. What do you feel?
- Now blow on your other forearm.

What's Up

When the water in sweat evaporates, or turns into a gas, it takes away heat. Rubbing alcohol evaporates even faster than water, so you can feel the effects right away. For this reason, blowing on the forearm that's wet with alcohol should have felt much cooler than the dry forearm. If you didn't notice this, maybe the alcohol evaporated so fast it was gone before you blew on it. Try using more alcohol on the cotton ball.

With the help of a partner, here's a variation on the experiment. You'll need two cotton balls and some water. With your partner's eyes closed, swipe one forearm with water and the other with alcohol. Gently blow on the moistened areas of the arms. Ask your partner which arm felt cooler. Remember, alcohol evaporates faster than water.

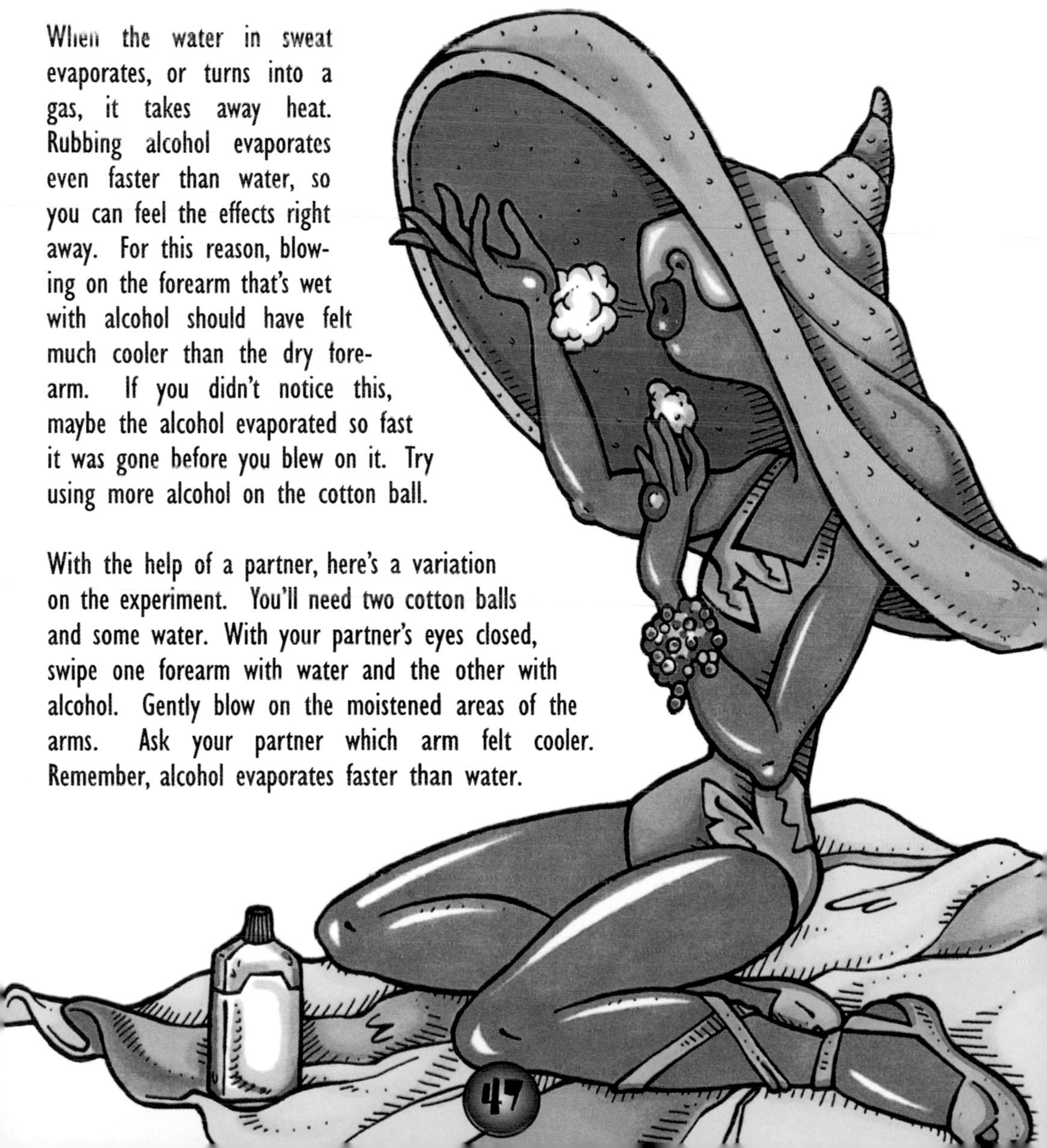

Right now you are breathing. At least you'd better be! (Or you won't be reading this book for very long.)

Humans constantly breathe. In fact, they can't survive for long at all without taking in air. Your breathing is fairly constant at about 12 breaths a minute. It slows when you sleep and speeds up when you exercise. Most breathing is *not* noticeable. However, if you eat a garlic-and-onion pizza or don't brush your teeth often enough—PHEUW!—your breathing *will* be noticed by others.

What you need:

a calculator or pencil and paper

What you do:

- You breathe about 12 times each minute. To determine how many times you breathe in an hour, multiply 12 by 60.
- Multiply that answer by 24 for the number of breaths in a day.
- Multiply that answer by 365 to find out how often you breathe in a year.
- Multiply that answer by your age to calculate the number of breaths you've taken in your life.
- The amount of air in one breath is about one-half of a liter.
- To figure out how many liters of air you breathe in one minute, multiply the number of breaths that you take in one minute by .5.
- Use the answers from your earlier calculations to determine how many liters of air you expel each hour, day, year, and up to now in your life.
- The next time you're in the soft-drink section of the grocery store, notice how many liters you breathe in one hour.

What's Up

The amount that you calculated for the breaths in your lifetime should be a very large number! If the number is not in the millions, try your calculations again. Remember that the numbers you calculated are not exact, since your breathing rate varies depending upon how active you are.

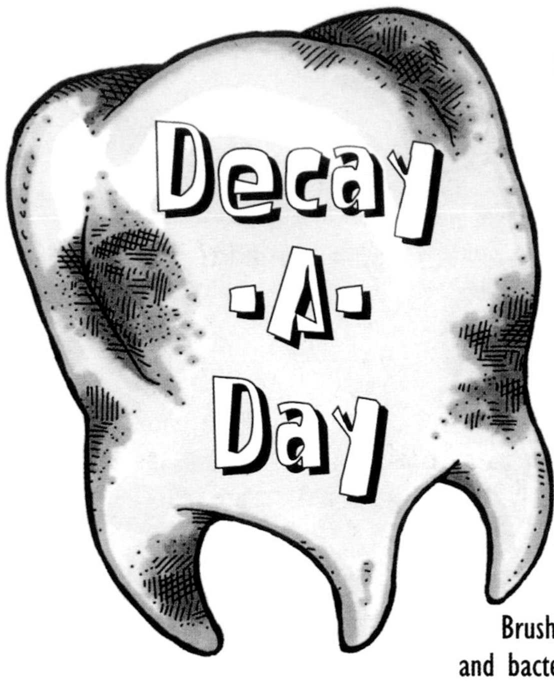

So you love to go to the dentist? You enjoy the sound, smell, and feel of a drill digging its way through your teeth. No? Then why don't you brush and floss regularly?!

It takes three things to make a ***cavity***: a tooth, food bits, and bacteria. First, the bacteria feed on the food bits (especially sugar). Bacteria then change the sugar to acid (pretty strong stuff that disintegrates your tooth). Next come cavities. Then comes drilling!

Brushing and flossing minimize these food bits and bacteria.

What you need:

cola

jar with a lid

a tooth (one that is not attached to a mouth); an eggshell can be substituted

calendar

What to do:

- Pour some cola in the jar and drop in the tooth.
- Cover the jar and place it in a safe spot. Mark the date on a calendar.
- Once each week, remove the tooth and observe.
- Continue checking the tooth for several weeks. What do you notice?

What's Up

The acid in the cola acts like the acid that bacteria forms in your mouth. The tooth in the jar begins to disintegrate as the acid eats away at the tooth's surface.

When you drink, cola passes through your mouth so quickly that it can't stage a direct acid attack (like the cola in the jar did). The only way it can directly destroy your teeth would be if you kept a gulp of cola in your mouth for several weeks. Hmmmm, that would be pretty hard to do.

If you didn't notice any change in the tooth, continue the experiment for a longer period of time. You may also want to use fresh cola, especially if the liquid in the jar is getting disgusting.

Booger-Picking Survey

Seventy out of every one hundred people admit to picking their nose.

Well, at least those are the results from one study. Conduct your own survey to determine the nose-picking rate in your community. You'll need a chart like this:

Booger-Picking Survey Chart

Person Asked	Picker	Non-Picker	Eater	Non-Eater

What you need:

paper

pencil

volunteers

Rhinotillexomania. Yep, that is the fancy, scientific word for nose picking.

What you do:

- On the paper make a chart as shown.
- Find a volunteer.
- Say "I am conducting a survey. Is it OK to ask a couple of questions?" Promise your volunteer that the survey is anonymous. (This means no one will ever know who you asked or how they answered. Keep your promise—forever!)
- Note each volunteer in the "Person Asked" column. The first person would be #1, the second #2, and so on.
- Ask your volunteer, "Do you pick your nose?"
- For a "yes" response, place an "x" in the "Picker" column. For a "no" response, place an "x" in the "Non-picker" column.
- If the volunteer is a nonpicker, say "Thank you for taking part in this important scientific survey."
- If your volunteer is a picker, ask "Do you eat them?" Place an "x" in the appropriate column. Then thank your volunteer.
- Continue your survey until you've questioned 25 people.
- Tally your results. How many pickers did you have? Out of your total number of pickers, how many were eaters?

What's Up

In a study conducted on nose picking, it was determined that out of 100 people, 70 will admit to picking their nose. Out of the 70 pickers, 3 will admit to eating them. Since you didn't ask 70 people, your results may show 17 or 18 pickers and 0 or 1 eaters.

If your results do not match these, that's fine. Maybe nose picking is not common in your area or, worse yet, maybe it is *very* common. Maybe your volunteers were all young or all old (nose-picking habits tend to change with age).

During your survey, you may have encountered some odd replies, such as "Does picking with a hankie count?" Yes. "Well, I used to eat them. Does that count?" This is your call. "Is blowing them out the same as picking?" No. "I would prefer not to answer." Don't count that person on your survey.

Toilet-Paper Testing

You use it everyday but you probably don't think much about it—toilet paper. Unless you're stuck without it. Then you think a lot about how much you miss having it.

Yet before it was invented by the Scott brothers in 1879, people didn't miss it. People just used other stuff. Now toilet paper is a standard item in most homes. Due to the great demand for toilet paper, many different brands are available for you to choose from. So, which toilet paper is the best? Try this experiment.

What you need:

several brands of toilet paper

water

dropper

a dozen large nuts or bolts

What you do:

To Test Absorbency

- From each brand of toilet paper, remove 3 squares.
- For each brand, fold the squares along the perforations to make 1 square. You now have 1 square per brand, which is 3 layers thick.
- Using the dropper, place a drop of water on each brand.
- Count to 10 and then check the bottom layer of each brand to see if water leaked through. Add water drop by drop to each brand until one leaks.
- The first brand to leak is the least absorbent. The one that holds the most drops before leaking is the most absorbent.

To Test for Strength

- Remove 1 square from each brand.
- Wet the center of each square.
- Place 1 nut or bolt upon each square. Lift. Do any of the brands rip?
- Add nuts or bolts until one of the brands rips when it is lifted.
- The brand to rip first is the least strong, the one to rip last is the strongest.

If the toilet paper kept ripping during the strength test, find a volunteer to help you. Have the volunteer hold one sheet of toilet paper as if it were a canopy. Then you add the water and the nuts or bolts to the center.

Just because one brand is more absorbent or stronger than another doesn't mean it is the best. The brand you use at home may be the cheapest, made from recycled paper, or the softest. Strength and absorbency are only two features that may help you to decide which toilet paper you want to use.

The Living Roach Motel

The English word for cockroach came from the Spanish name "cucaracha." In Spanish, *cuca* is the word for caterpillar and *acha* means "contemptible." So, cockroaches have not been on the list of adorable critters for many years, regardless of one's language.

However, this insect with a brain in its head and a simple brain in its behind is really not so bad. Cockroaches are quite clean, and they will eat most anything. If you want to better appreciate roaches, try this experiment.

WARNING: DO THIS EXPERIMENT ONLY WITH PARENTAL APPROVAL. THIS BOOK'S CREATORS AND PUBLISHER DO NOT TAKE ANY RESPONSIBILITY FOR THE CONSEQUENCES OF A RUNAWAY COCKROACH.

What you need:

petroleum jelly

paper plate

plastic shoe box with holes in the lid or a small fish tank with a lid

small, shallow dish or jar lid

water

sponge

various foods

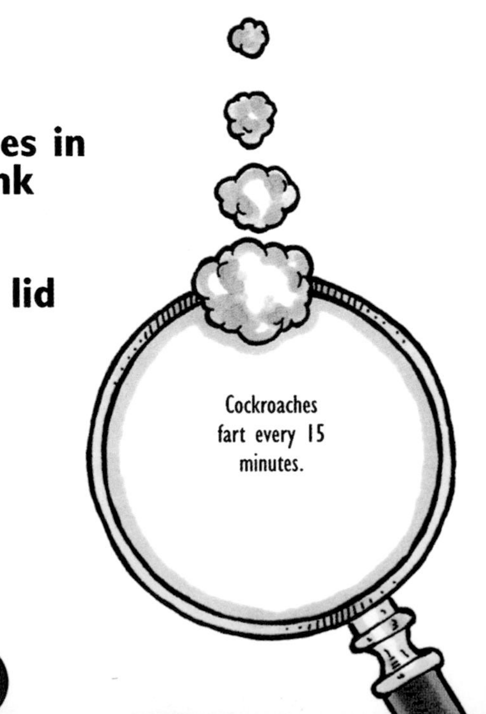

What you do:

Catch A Roach

- Smear a layer of petroleum jelly over the plate.
- Add some yummy food such as white bread or cinnamon rolls to the plate.
- Find a roachy area. If you don't have any at home, try outside behind a restaurant or near a stack of wood. (Be careful to not announce your plan at the restaurant, as the customers would prefer to enjoy their meal.)
- Leave plate overnight; check it in the morning.

Construct A Roach Motel

- Clean your roach home (the shoe box or fish tank).
- Place the dish into the roach home.
- Pour water into the dish to cover the bottom, then place the sponge in the water.
- Decorate the home with cardboard hiding spots.
- After you catch a cockroach, put it in the roach home. If you caught several roaches, quickly prepare a home for each roach or choose your favorite roach and keep it. Let it get adjusted. You will know your new friend is calm and adjusted to life in its new little world when it slows down.

Experiment—Have Fun

- Name your cockroach friend.
- Feed your cockroach various types of food to find out which it prefers. Treat your cockroach kindly, and DON'T LET IT OUT IN THE HOUSE!

If you don't catch a cockroach, you can purchase cockroaches from several biological supply companies. Your teacher will probably have catalogs from one of these companies. Roaches need water, so make sure you add water to the dish occasionally. Be careful to not overfill the dish, as your roach could drown while trying to get a drink. Healthy cockroaches can live from several months to several years.
So, be prepared for a long relationship.

Moldy Bread

There's a ***fungus*** among us! In the refrigerator! In the bathroom! In your bedroom!

Fungus is also known as mold or mildew. Usually, you never see a single fungus. Any one fungus is quite small (microscopic!). What you see growing in your cottage cheese is a *whole bunch* of fungus. You see fungi (FUN jeye). And they are busily eating up almost everything they land upon.

Where do you think bread mold grows best? In the dark or in lots of light? Not sure? Then check out this experiment.

What you need:

2 slices of bread

2 resealable plastic bags

water

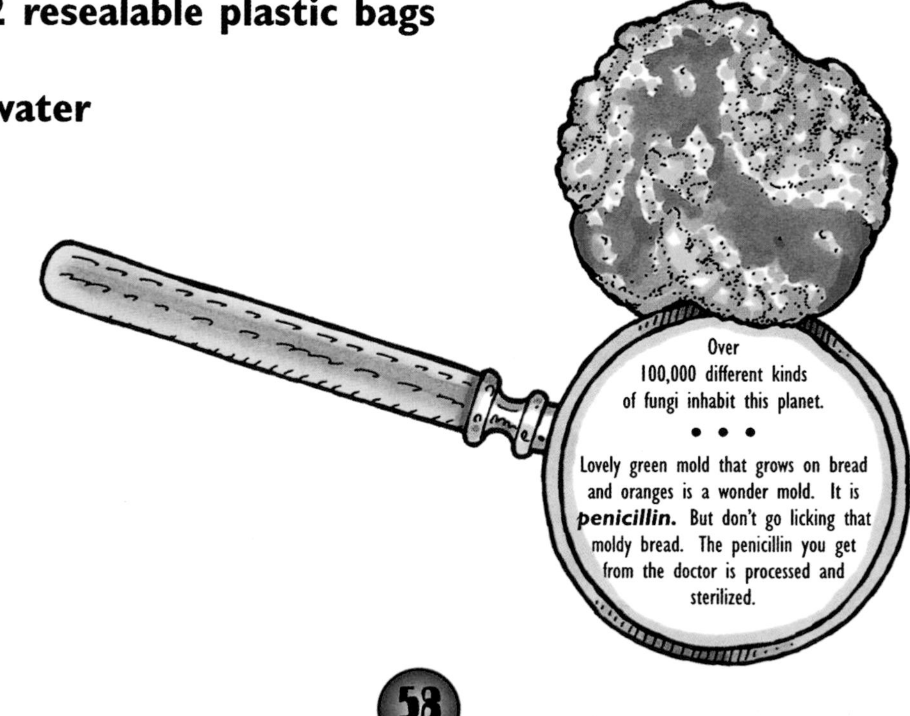

Over 100,000 different kinds of fungi inhabit this planet.

• • •

Lovely green mold that grows on bread and oranges is a wonder mold. It is ***penicillin.*** But don't go licking that moldy bread. The penicillin you get from the doctor is processed and sterilized.

What you do:

- Place a slice of bread in each bag. (If you want lots of mold, rub each slice in a dusty area before placing it in the bag.)
- Using your fingers, sprinkle water onto each slice of bread. Don't soak the bread, just dampen it.
- Close each bag.
- Place one bag in a dark area and the other in a sunny or well-lit area.
- After 5 days, check each bag.
- Which bag was home to the most furry friends? Discard the bags after you show them to your great aunt.

You probably discovered that more mold grew on the bread that was kept in the dark. Mold likes warm, dark, damp places. That is why houses often rot first underneath, rather than on the sunny roof.

If nothing grew on your bread, check to see if the bread is hard. Dry bread means you did not add enough water before you sealed the bags. Repeat the experiment using more water. Very mushy bread means you added too much water. Repeat the experiment using less water.

Mold also likes warmth. You may lack fungi growth if your bread was placed in a cold area. Repeat the experiment and place one bag in a warm, sunny spot and the other in a warm, dark spot.

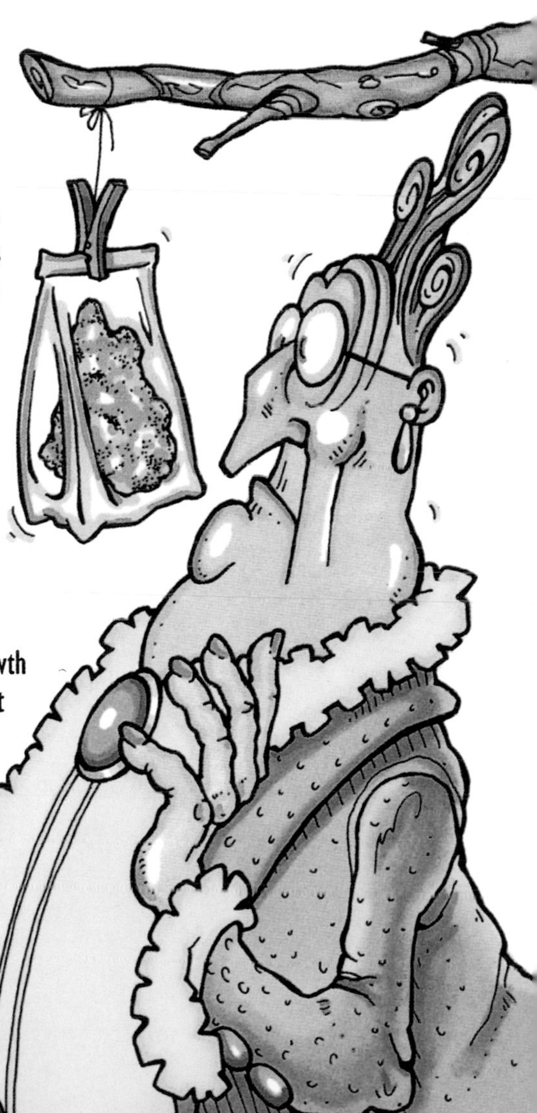

You tip the milk over a bowl of cereal. Lump, glump, lump. Yuck! Or you raise a glass of milk to your mouth and swallow. Ack! Sour!

Don't blame the bad milk on the cow; blame it on bacteria. Even a fresh carton of milk contains some bacteria. The bacteria reproduce in the milk but you don't notice it. However, after about a week, milk begins to sour from all the bacteria pee pee. Eventually, the milk proteins stick together to form white curdled lumps.

To determine if warmth or cold makes bacteria turn milk sour faster, try this gross experiment.

What you need:

milk

a glass

2 small jars with lids

refrigerator

What you do:

- Pour milk into glass.
- Leave the glass of milk out for several hours, until the milk warms to room temperature. WARNING: TAPE A "DO NOT DRINK" SIGN TO THE GLASS.
- Pour half of the milk into 1 jar. Cover and place that jar in the refrigerator (WARNING: check with a parent to make sure that no one drinks this half of your experiment).
- Pour the rest of the milk into the other jar. Cover and place this jar in a warm place (WARNING: again, make sure your parents know you're doing this and make *real* sure that no one drinks this half of your experiment).
- Check the milk after a couple of days. Notice anything?
- Look at it again after a week. (Do *not* smell the milk at this point—it could really stink in a sickening way!) Discard both jars.

What's Up

The jar of milk in the warm spot sours more quickly than the milk jar in the cold. Bacteria enjoy heat. In a warm environment, they reproduce quickly.

If your milk doesn't curdle, let it sit for several more days. If after the extended waiting period there's still no curdling, your experiment may be short on bacteria. Try the experiment again. This time leave the glass of milk out for longer before dividing it into the two jars. Another problem could be that you have the second jar in a spot that's too cold. Try a warmer place.

Grow Your Own Bacteria

They're everywhere! No, not space aliens. Bacteria!

Bacteria are living on your face, munching in your intestines, swimming in the sink, and mating in your bathroom. Yep, the tiny world of bacteria surrounds you.

Many people refer to bacteria as germs. ***Germs*** are bad. Bacterial germs cause illnesses like food poisoning (***salmonella***) and strep throat (***streptococcus***). But some bacteria are helpful (they're not called germs). Bacteria live in your gut, breaking down food and making vitamin K. And without bacteria, life would be less tasty. Yep, thank good ol' bacteria for cheese and yogurt.

What you need:

distilled water (distilled works best, but tap water is OK)

measuring cup

a pot with a lid

a chicken boullion cube

sugar

spoon

3 very clean bowls

plastic wrap

What you do:

STOP! GET AN ADULT! PROCEED TO THE STOVE ONLY WITH AN ADULT!

- Measure 3 cups of water into a pot. Bring the water to a boil.
- Add the boullion cube and 1 spoonful of sugar.
- Allow the mixture to boil for several minutes.
- After boiling, cover the pot and remove from heat.
- Pour equal amounts of the boullion mixture into each bowl.
- Pick three different spots to place the bowls. (On the back of the toilet, near the garbage, or by the kitchen sink are good spots. Or try coughing into a bowl, dabbing your fingers in another, and leaving one alone.)
  WARNING: TAPE "DO NOT EAT OR DRINK!" SIGNS TO EACH BOWL. BE SURE YOUR PARENTS KNOW ABOUT THIS EXPERIMENT.
- After one day, cover the bowls with plastic wrap and place them in a warm place where nobody will mess with your experiment.
- Check after one week to see what's grown.

What's Up

If bacteria are present, the liquid will be cloudy. Clear broth means that nothing grew. Maybe the bowls were stored in a cool spot or maybe you placed the uncovered bowls in a low-bacteria zone. Try again.

Owl Pellets

If you were an owl and had eaten dinner almost a day ago, you'd now be getting ready to *raaalf!* And that would be good.

Owls swallow their dinner (a mouse, for example) whole. They have no teeth, so they just gulp without chewing. Strong stomach chemicals dissolve the soft parts of dinner, but the hard parts remain. Because the opening from the stomach to the intestine is too small to let the hard bits fit through to the other end, the only choice is to bring the stuff back up through the mouth.

Owl vomits are called owl pellets. Inside a pellet are complete skeletons of the animals that served as dinner. Scientists dissect pellets for information about the health of an environment. The owl pellets reveal the variety of small mammals that live in an area. And variety is an indicator of an environmentally healthy area.

What you need:

rubber gloves

an owl pellet
(If you know the location of an owl nest, search the ground, and collect your own pellets. Or you can purchase owl-pellet kits at many educational toy stores)

sheet of white paper

tweezers

long needle

glue

cardboard

What you do:

- PUT ON THE RUBBER GLOVES.
- Place the pellet on the sheet of paper.
- Use the tweezers and needle to separate the bones.
- Collect the bones in a pile.
- Sort the bones into skulls, backbones, legs, and so on.
- Choose the bones that you think belong to one animal.
- Piece the bones together to form a skeleton.
- Glue the skeleton onto cardboard.
- Throw away the fur and other animal parts that you don't use.
- After you are done, THOROUGHLY AND CAREFULLY wash your hands.

What's Up

If it's difficult separating the bones from the fur and other debris, first soak the pellet in water for several hours.

Once you've separated the bones as suggested (a skull pile, a jaw pile, and another pile of ribs), pull from each pile the largest or the tiniest of each type. These will probably belong to the same animal. A book (check your public or school library) with illustrations of rodent or bird skeletons will help you re-create the skeleton of the animal that served as dinner. Remember that an owl sometimes eats a whole lot for dinner. Your owl pellet may contain the skeleton of just one dinner tidbit, or it may have the bones from as many as six critters.

Pet Slime Molds

They are creeping blobs of slime. They are alive. They are harmless. They are slime molds.

Envision a giant loogie that spreads out. Basically, that is how most slime molds look: shiny, slimy, and yucky. (Moreover, some slime molds can also be quite pretty. One type resembles glistening orange or yellow strands that creep out into a fanlike shape.)

Slime molds choose damp, decaying places to live. They can be found anywhere that rot takes place, such as under forest leaves, near a swamp, or in the dirt. Cold weather is not their favorite. So, it is best to conduct a slime mold search during warm seasons.

What you need:

damp paper towel in a plastic bag

large bowl-shaped coffee filter

small bowl

a jar that is large enough to place the bowl on its bottom

water

ground oatmeal

lid or plate to cover the opening of the jar

paper towels

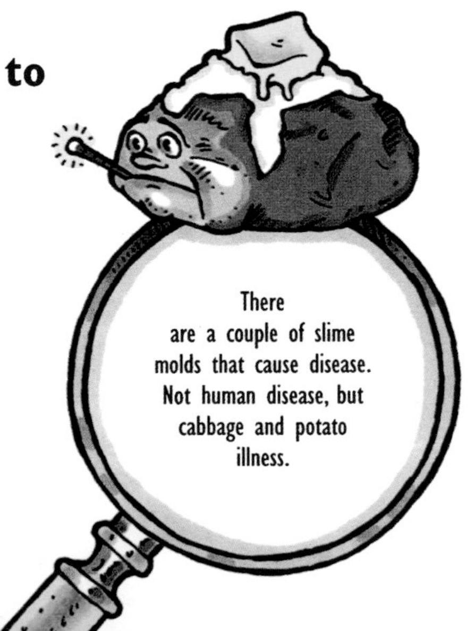

What you do:

- Search under rotting logs, fallen leaves, and dead twigs for a slimy blob or veinlike creature.
- When you find a slime mold, place your new pet into the plastic bag. Don't remove your new friend from its leaf or decaying wood—just place the wood or leaf in the bag too.
- Wrap the coffee filter around the small bowl to make a drum.
- Make sure the filter paper is flat on the top of the bowl.
- Place this small bowl with coffee filter paper into the large jar.
- Pour water down the interior side of the large jar until water just touches the bottom edge of the coffee filter.
- Place your new pet onto the flat top of the coffee filter drum.
- Feed your slime mold a pinch of ground oatmeal.
- Cover the jar with a lid or a plate to keep out flies.
  WARNING: PUT A "DO NOT EAT OR DRINK ANYTHING IN HERE" SIGN ON THE JAR
- Feed your slimy pet every day or two. If the water level falls below the bottom of the coffee filter, add water until it once again touches the filter.
- If your mold spreads to cover the filter paper, it will need more creeping surface. Using paper towels, line the walls of the jar. Leave some glass clear so you can easily check on your pet.
- Love your slime mold and don't forget to name it.

What's Up

Finding a slime mold is the hardest part of this experiment. Slime molds like to live in rotten areas like the forest floor or a swamp. Check under leaves or on rotting logs. If you see a spot that looks like a giant loogie, you have located a slime mold. The best slime mold-hunting seasons are the spring or fall. Good luck.

Snails probably don't show up on many people's list of lovable animals. But they really are fascinating creatures.

Snails can be found sliming along from the snow line to beneath the sea. Snails like damp places, but they can survive without water by hiding out inside their shells. They actually plug up their shell opening to seal themselves off.

Try this experiment and maybe you'll actually grow fond of the slimy little critters.

What you need:

snail

a sheet of clear, hard plastic (anything smaller than 10 inches by 10 inches won't be much fun)

lettuce

pebbles or marbles

What you do:

- Find a snail. Morning or evening is usually the best time to go snail hunting. (Snails really like gardens.)
- Lift the snail gently by the shell.
- Place snail on the plastic sheet.
- Hold up plastic to observe the snail as it crawls. If the snail won't move, place some lettuce at one end of the plastic.
- Place objects in the path of the snail.
- Watch the snail glide across the objects. Observe from above and below the snail.
- If you feel really brave, place the snail on your hand. Feel the creature slime across your palm.
- Return the animal to a moist area. Away from your garden would be the best bet, as snails love to munch vegetables and certain flowers. However, they are quite happy eating the grass and wild flowers that don't need tending like the garden.

What's Up

Finding a snail may be a little difficult. The best time of year is during the spring or summer. The best location is in a garden. Some gardeners guard against snails. Check with the gardener first to make sure that snails are present. If all else fails, you may be able to purchase snails from a fresh seafood market. People actually eat snails! When you eat them, snails are called *escargots*.

Some people become very attached to their snails and want to keep them. If you just can't give up your snail, place the little critter into a jar or plastic shoe box. Make sure your pet has air holes. Snails need calcium to keep their shells strong. An easy-to-find source of calcium is chalk. Place a small piece of chalk in the home. Give Herbert some water and lots of fresh vegetables.

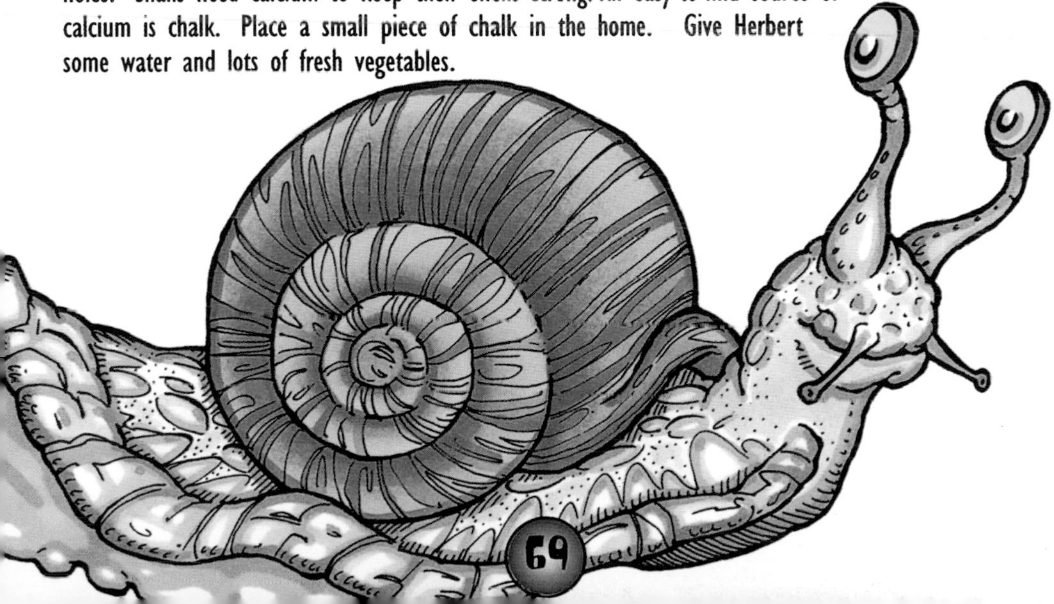

An Important Note to Teachers

The goal of grossology—the science of really gross things—is not to be gross, but to teach science.

In a traditional introductory science course, children are expected to learn more vocabulary than they are in a first-year language course. All that newly obtained vocabulary is then coupled with new concepts. The child must translate the new words and immediately apply them. Because this is so difficult to do, many children, regretfully, learn only to hate science.

Grossology, however, presents scientific information without burying it under layers of vocabulary. Common words are used to present concepts. Although scientific terms are also introduced, the child is not dependent upon them for understanding a complex process. (However, the value of enriching a child's scientific vocabulary should not be overlooked. In each Grossology book, new terms are boldfaced, pronunciations are given, and definitions provided. This book contains a Gross Glossary beginning on page 75. The objective of the glossary is not to present the students with a list of terms to memorize but to allow for easy access to increasing their scientific vocabulary.)

Grossology was created by a science educator (me!). One day, as I sat clipping my toenails, an idea hit me: "Kids love gross stuff. That's it! I can teach them science using gross as a hook. And I'll call this new science—the science of really gross things—'grossology!' "

What about parents or the administration?

Parental disapproval has not been a problem for teachers using the Grossology Series. Kids become so excited about learning the information that they often share their newly acquired knowledge at home. When the parents see how thrilled their children are about learning science, buy-in is not a problem.

It is a good idea to check with your administration before using grossology resources in the classroom. With the establishment of the Grossology Series as a legitimate science resource, administrative hesitation is virtually nonexistent. However, in a few cases, principals request that teachers refrain from discussing certain sections, such as farts or boogers.

I was soon able to test text materials and various activities on students in my after-school science program. (They were hooked!) Then in the classroom—where I taught science to kindergarten through high school—I tested additional materials on my junior high kids. Soon, fellow teachers overheard junior high students sharing the information with younger students. The concept worked even better than I had imagined.

These tested and proven materials eventually grew into the Grossology Series, a series of books (see page 80) that explore the science of grossology. The first book of the series, **Grossology**, is a human physiology and health book. **Animal Grossology** focuses on zoology and animal physiology. The integrated science book of the series is **Grossology Begins at Home**. It contains health science, human and animal physiology, ecology, and even a bit of physical science.

Then there is this book, **Hands-On Grossology**. The focus of this book is experience. Although some background information is presented with each activity, it is less information-driven than the other three books. In hundreds of e-mails and letters, at lectures and speaking engagements, at NSTA conferences and science museums throughout North America, educators were constantly seeking new ways to present science, which led people to me. Yet I was often asked for copies of various gross activities or for ideas on how to supplement the material with experiences. So, here it is—**Hands-On Grossology**.

With **Hands-On Grossology**, you now have the complete resources to use grossology in the classroom. You'll see that the book has three sections (see "Table of Grosstents," page 3): "Fake Grossness," "Your Personal Gross Experiments," and "Gross Experiments from All Around." Let's take a quick look at each of those sections.

Fake Grossness

(pages 8 – 25)

Kids learn best by doing. Once a child is exposed to a concept, the "doing" further embeds the learning. The act of doing may take on various forms such as reproducing, discovering, modeling, observing, calculating, and open exploring.

Fake grossness activities produce imitations of the real thing or models of events that take place inside of the body. These activities help children to apply information they have learned. A child making a fake wound must think about how a real wound actually feels and looks: the child creates a model of what exists in the actual world. As the experience takes place, the information previously presented becomes reinforced. If the activity takes place before the information, the curiosity of the child is higher. Thus, retention of the information is greater as well.

Best of all, making fake gross stuff is really fun. (It can also be a bit messy, so you may want to cover the desks with newspaper.)

Note: After completing the activities for fake poo, blood, snot, barf, and dookie cookies, store the fake grossness until the close of the day. Otherwise, kids will fuss with the fascinating stuff. (Or you could schedule the activities for the end of the day.)

Your Personal Gross Experiments (pages 26 – 51)

Kids of all ages are fascinated with themselves. For middle schoolers, their rapidly changing bodies draw their attention. Although many of these changes are specific to certain areas, the body fascination is not. They are just as intrigued with learning about spit as they are learning about puberty.

Yet if you asked your students, "Raise your hand if you want to learn about the excretory system," few students would respond. But if you asked, "Raise your hand if you want to learn about pee, poo, and sweat," many enthusiastic hands would go up. That is the teaching approach used by grossology: the kids are actually studying human physiology and health, but they don't know it.

Many of the experiments in "Your Personal Gross Experiments" can be performed in the classroom. However, experiments that involve poop or pee should be discoveries that are made at home and not in school. You may wish to assign them as homework or as extra credit.

The more children understand their bodies, the better they take care of them. "Your Personal Gross Experiments" is the perfect opportunity to introduce kids to the fascinating world of themselves.

Gross Experiments from All Around

(pages 52 – 69)

If children can relate information to their everyday lives, they will retain the information longer. The Grossology Series was developed with this in mind. The scientific topics are cloaked in familiar settings. For example, in **Animal Grossology**, sea lampreys are discussed. Most students will never encounter a lamprey. However, this animal is included in a section titled "Slime Makers." Students can relate to slime. They may also be familiar with other animals of slime, such as slugs or snails.

In "Gross Experiments from All Around," students experience the exploration of animals they may encounter daily but overlook, such as snails, mold, and bacteria. By creating a meaningful experience with common objects and animals, the world opens up for the students. Kids begin to question and seek answers in their "everyday" experiences. Keen observation skills are key to the success of many people, including scientists. These simple experiments begin to focus the students on developing their observation skills.

All of the materials (even the critters) are common to every geographic area. However, collecting some of the materials may be dependent upon the seasons. Worry not. Snails, owl pellets, slime molds, and cockroaches are available from many scientific supply companies.

A Gross Glossary

acid (ASS id) A sharp, biting, sour chemical. Sometimes acids irritate and wear out other substances.

antacid (ANT ASS id) The "ant" part comes from "anti," which means "against." So an antacid is a chemical that acts against an acid. Usually antacids are medicines taken for an upset stomach. They change the belly acid to gas and a less irritating liquid.

antiperspirants (AN ti PUR spir ant) "Anti" means "against." "Perspire" means "to sweat." An antiperspirant is a product that people put on their armpits to help reduce the amount of sweat that comes from the sweat pores.

anus (AY nus) This is the scientific term for the exit opening from your butt where your poop comes out.

bacteria (back TEER e a) Some people incorrectly call these germs. They are actually one-celled living creatures found almost everywhere. Some types are helpful to humans and other kinds make us sick.

bladder (BLAD er) This is the pee pee storage sack. It is like a balloon that stretches as it fills with pee and collapses when it is emptied.

blister (BLIS ter) A sore, caused by liquid collecting between layers of skin, which results in a little bubble-like bump.

cavity (CAV i tee) An empty place. In the case of your teeth, a cavity is a hole in your tooth caused by the destructive bacteria waste that eats away at the enamel.

constipation (con sta PAY shun) When you can't poop.

cross linker (CROSS link er) A type of molecule that joins together the long strands of another type of molecule.

deodorants (dee O door ant) "De" means to "remove from." A deodorant removes odor, or smell, from somebody or something. With people, deodorants kill the bacteria that live in the armpits.

excretory (X cree tore ee) The parts of the body that get rid of waste. The excretory system includes the organs that cause pooping, peeing, sweating, and getting rid of carbon dioxide (the stuff that you breathe out).

erythrocytes (a RITH ra sites) The scientific term for red blood cells.

fungus (FUN gus) A plantlike organism that feeds and lives on its food source. Commonly called mildew or mold.

germs (jurms) The common word for bacteria and viruses that cause illness.

grossology (gross OL o gee) The science of really gross things.

grossologist (gross OL o gist) A person who scientifically studies really gross things.

heartburn (HART burn) When stomach acids back up into your throat and cause a burning sensation. The burning often feels like it is near your heart but heartburn actually has nothing to do with your heart.

hemoglobin (HE ma globe in) The iron-containing pigment in red blood cells.

infection (in FEK shun) When foreign invaders like bacteria or fungi get into an area of your body and take up housekeeping. Often doctors give you medicine to kill off the invaders and end the infection.

iodine (I o dine) A pure chemical element; iodine dissolved in alcohol is used to treat cuts.

kidney (KID nee) An organ in your body that filters your blood. The kidney separates the waste from blood. You then pee out that waste.

large intestine (in TES tin) A tube in your gut that removes some water from mushed-up food before forming it into individual poops.

lockjaw (LOCK jaw) A disease which causes the jaw muscles to spasm so that the mouth gets locked shut.

maggot (MAG it) The wormlike stage in the life of a fly. Yuck!

penicillin (pen a SILL in) A type of medicine (antibiotic) used to treat infections. Penicillin is made by a special mold.

peristalsis (pear a STAL sis) Movement of your intestinal muscles as they send processed food and water through your intestines.

peristaltic (pear a STAL tic) rush A fancy word for pooping.

perspiration (PUR spir a shun) Sweat.

plaque (plack) A layer of scum that forms over your teeth. It is a mixture of food bits, mouth cells, bacteria, and bacteria waste.

polymer (POLL i mer) A type of long molecule made of simple parts repeated over and over then strung together.

proctologist (prok TALL a gist) A medical doctor that specializes in problems of the poop system.

raptors (RAP tors) Birds of prey with keen eyesight and sharp claws that hunt for their food.

rectum (RECK tum) Your butthole.

salivary (SAL a very) amylase (AM a lace) The chemical in your spit that breaks up starch molecules and turns them into sugar.

salivary (SAL a very) glands (glands) Little organs in your mouth that squirt out spit.

saliva (sa LI va) Spit; breaks down food when you chew and helps you to swallow.

salmonella (sal ma NELL a) Bacteria that cause food poisoning.

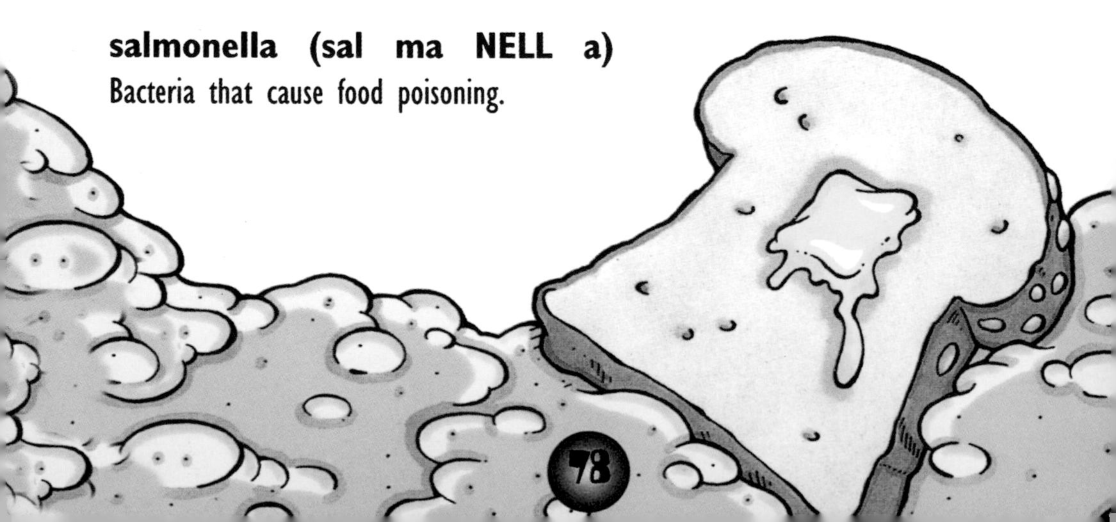

scat (scat) Wild animal poop.

sebaceous (sa BAY shus) glands (glands) Little sacks under your skin that squirt out oils.

small intestine (in TES tin) A long tube in your gut that collects nutrients from your food.

starch (starch) A substance in plants that is found in much of our food, such as breads and cereals.

streptococcus (strep toe CAULK sis) Bacteria that cause strep throat.

tetanus (TET niss) Bacteria that cause lockjaw.

urea (yur EE a) A waste product produced by your cells and released in your pee.

vaccinations (vak sa NAY shuns) Shots that doctors give you to protect you from various diseases.

vesicles (VES i culls) Very small blisters, like the kind you get with the chicken pox.

Other Tasteful Offerings from Price Stern Sloan's Grossology Series

GROSSOLOGY

The original gross classic! Sometimes it's crusty. Sometimes it's stinky. And sometimes it's slimy. Not the book—your body! And here's all the icky, oozing information about it, presented in the scientifically correct manner that has already grossed out millions.

GROSSOLOGY AND YOU

Picking up where Grossology left off, this further exploration of your body's most icky characteristics includes evrything from goosebumps to hiccups, constipation to knuckle cracking, and rashes to warts—all explained in kid-friendly, scientifically correct terms.